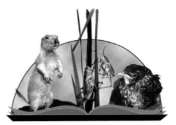

WE CAN READ about NATURE!™

by ANITA HOLMES

BENCHMARK BOOKS

MARSHALL CAVENDISH
NEW YORK

With thanks to
Lynn Holmes, zoologist, for reading the manuscript and
offering suggestions. Dr. Holmes teaches and lectures in
Los Angeles.

Benchmark Books
Marshall Cavendish Corporation
99 White Plains Road
Tarrytown, New York 10591

Photo research by Candlepants, Inc.

Cover photo: *The National Audubin Society Collection / Photo Researchers, Inc.,*
Rod Planck

The photographs in this book are used by permission and through the courtesy of:
The National Audubon Society Collection / Photo Researchers, Inc.: Ken M. Highfill, 4;
Gregory G. Dimijian, 5, 8 (bottom), 10-11; Dr. Paul A. Zahl, 6 (top); Ray Coleman, 6
(bottom); Stephen Dalton, 7 (top); Hermann Eisenbeiss, 7 (bottom); Jacana Scientific, 8
(top); Ken Cavanagh, 9 (top); Michael Lustbader, 9 (bottom), 28-29; Gary Retherford,
12; Science Source Library, 13; Bill Bachman, 14; Fletcher and Bayliss, 15; C.K. Lorenz,
16; Karl H. Switak, 17; David Schleser, 18; Stephen Dalton, 19 (top); Kjell Sandved, 19
(bottom); Harry Rogers, 20 (top); Gilbert Grant, 20 (bottom); Richard F. Trump, 21;
David T. Roberts, 22; George D. Lepp, 23; John Mitchell, 24, 25 (top), 25 (bottom);
Millard H. Sharp, 26,27.

Library of Congress Cataloging-in-Publication Data

Holmes, Anita, date
Insect detector / by Anita Holmes.
p. cm.— (We can read about nature!)
Includes index (p.32)
Summary: Simple information allows the reader to "detect" which of a variety
of creatures are actually insects.
ISBN 0-7614-1110-0
1. Insects—Juvenile literature. [1. Insects.] I. Title.
QL467.2.H654 2001   595.7—dc21   99-057016

Printed in Italy

1 3 5 6 4 2

Look for us inside this book.

ant
beetle
butterfly
cricket
dragonfly
grasshopper
honeybee
leafhopper
moth
praying mantis
stinkbug
water strider

The world is full of insects—
millions and millions of them.
They live almost everywhere
on Earth.

Monarch butterflies in Kansas

A shield bug in northern Australia

Most insects can crawl.

Beetles

Many insects
can fly.

A comet moth

6

Some insects
can hop.

A rhododendron leafhopper

A water strider

This insect can even walk on water.

Most insects are small.
But they work very hard.

Weaver ants

They carry big loads.

*Leafcutter
ants*

8

Some live together.

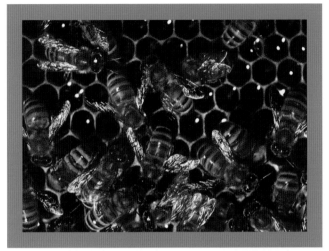

Honeybees

Others live alone.

A praying mantis

9

There are many kinds of insects.
How are all of them alike?
An insect must have a stiff skeleton.

Your skeleton is inside your body. An insect's wraps around the outside like a shell.

A red beetle

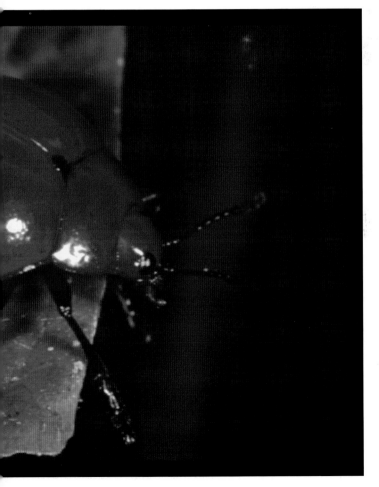

An insect's body has three parts: a head, a middle, and an abdomen. Insects have six legs with joints.

A black ant

A speckled bush cricket

They have two antennas.
They may have two or
four wings.

You are an insect detector.

This animal has a stiff
outside skeleton.
But it is not an insect.
Why not?

Insects have six legs. This spider has eight.

Here are two little hoppers.
Which one is an insect?
Which one is not?

*A leaf frog. Its skeleton is inside its body.
It has four legs and no antennas.*

A grasshopper. Its skeleton is outside its body. It has six legs and two antennas.

Here are a giant centipede,
a scorpion, and
two giraffe beetles.
Look closely.

A centipede

Two of them are insects.
(Count the legs!)
The other two are not.

A scorpion

Giraffe beetles

All insects hatch from eggs.

Stinkbug eggs

A praying mantis egg case

A monarch butterfly egg

Some newborns look like little adults when they hatch.

Newly hatched stinkbugs

A newborn mantis

Others go through
amazing changes.

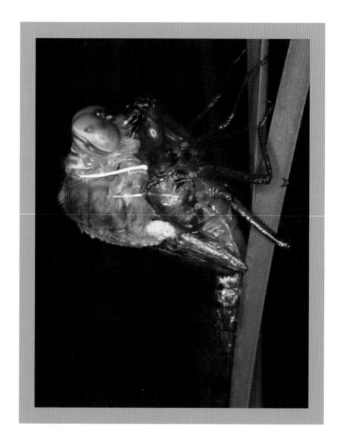

A young dragonfly
sheds its skin.

Out comes a grown-up.
Soon it will fly.

A caterpillar hangs from a leaf.

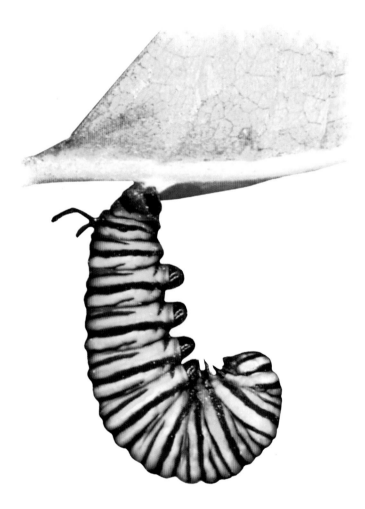

It forms a hard shell called a pupa.
One day the pupa cracks open.
Do you know what comes out?

27

A butterfly.

A monarch butterfly

fun with phonics

How do we become fluent readers? We interpret, or decode, the written word. Knowledge of phonics—the rules and patterns for pronouncing letters—is essential. When we come upon a word we cannot figure out by any other strategy, we need to sound out that word.

Here are some very effective tools to help early readers along their way. Use the "add-on" technique to sound out unknown words. Simply add one sound at a time, always pronouncing previous sounds. For instance, to sound out the word **cat**, first say **c**, then **c-a**, then **c-a-t**, and finally the entire word **cat**. Reading "chunks" of letters is another important skill. These are patterns of two or more letters that make one sound.

Words from this book appear below. The markings are clues to help children master phonics rules and patterns. All consonant sounds are circled. Single vowels are either long ‾, short ˘, or silent ╱. Have fun with phonics, and a fluent reader will emerge.

Short "u" words:

b ŭ t   b ŭ t t e r f l y ī   g r o‾ w n - ŭ p

m ŭ s t   s t ĭ n k b ŭ g

A word that begins with a vowel can make either a long or a short vowel sound. The reader will need to try both to see which sound makes sense.

a‾ d ŭ l t s   a‾ l o‾ n e   a‾ m a‾ z ĭ n g

a‾ n t   e‾ g g s   ī n s ĕ c t s

30

When the letters "en" are together, they say the letter name N.

ā̆ n̄ t ĕ n̄ n ā̆ s   ē̆ v ĕ n   ō̆ p ĕ n

When the letter "g" is followed by an "e" or an "i" it makes the / j / sound.

c h ā n g ē s   g ī ā n t   g i r ă f f ĕ

fun facts

- Scientists have discovered more than 1 million kinds of insects. More are being discovered every day.
- Each acre of earth holds more than 4 million insects.
- The world's biggest insect is the atlas moth of Asia. Its wings stretch 12 inches (30 cm) from tip to tip.
- The Goliath beetle of Africa is the world's heaviest insect. It is about 5 or 6 inches (13-15 cm) long and weighs more than 1.5 ounces (42 g).
- Some insects can fly very fast. Some can beat their wings 1,000 times per second.

glossary/index

about the author

Anita Holmes is both a writer and an editor with a long career in children's and educational publishing. She has a special interest in nature, gardening, and the environment and has written numerous articles and books for children on these subjects. A number of her books have won commendations from the American Library Association, the National Science Teachers Association, and The New York Public Library. She lives in Norfolk, Connecticut.